❄ winter grilling

Printed in Canada

Cataloguing in Publication data available from Library and Archives Canada
ISBN: 978-1-77050-249-9

14 15 16 17 18   5 4 3 2 1

The publisher acknowledges the financial support of the Government of Canada through the Canada Book Fund (CBF) and the Province of British Columbia through the Book Publishing Tax Credit.

 This book was printed on chlorine-free paper made with 10% post-consumer waste.

winter grilling

Tom Heinzle

whitecap

contents

wintertime: grill time

Nowadays, grilling and barbecuing are more popular than ever—and the trend shows no signs of abating. When the weather's warm—whether it's a casual affair in a backyard or at a lake, whether it's on a hiking trail or on a comfortable terrace—you'll find grills everywhere.

Hardly any type of food preparation will evoke your guests' astonishment and enthusiasm quite the way grilling and barbecuing do. Hosts know from experience, as well as from specialty magazines, books and grill courses, that grilling is a great way to unwind.

In our latitudes, we tend to think of the winter months as a time to enjoy quiet, rest and recuperation. That's exactly why, in my view, this is the perfect time for grilling. The time when sumptuous dishes find their way onto the grill to be infused with the wonderful aromas of winter.

This is the season to rediscover old, traditional vegetables. But beef, pork, lamb, poultry and fish can also be prepared in absolutely delicious ways with winter spices and side dishes. Winter grilling is thus an opportunity to bring completely new flavour combinations to the table.

With this book, dear reader, I'd like to show you that winter doesn't mean a compulsory break from grilling and barbecuing. The beginning of the colder season simply means the advent of a grilling season that until now has been all too ignored and neglected. An enormous variety of products available in these months lend themselves to being prepared and refined on the grill. In this book, I've tried to include all commonly used types of grill. The recipes can be used for wood, coal or gas grills.

In this spirit, I hope that this book will delight and inspire you.

With fiery-smoky greetings,

Your Tom Heinzle

thanks

I would like to thank my wife and two sons for the patience they extend toward me so that I can forge ahead in the grill circus.

Special thanks go to my wife, Claudia, who is my constant inspiration to discover new combinations and recipes and who, through her constructive criticism, always pushes me to top-notch achievements at the grill and smoker. I'd also like to thank the team at Tom's Grillwerkstatt (Tom's Grill Workshop) and all my partners, who support me and have always believed in me. I hope that will continue to be the case. Thanks to Christine and Michael for transforming my ideas into this book, and thanks to my family and friends, and, of course, everybody who's taken part in my grill courses and demonstrations and anyone who will do so in the future.

what you should know

Grilling in winter, as opposed to the balmy summer, is much more demanding of not only the person manning the grill but also the grill itself. From the outside, warm, functional clothing can protect the grill master from the icy temperatures. From the inside, hot tea or mulled wine can help keep the cold at bay.

When it comes to the equipment, it's a bit different. In winter, a gas grill uses significantly more gas than in summer. For this reason, I deliberately position my gas grill in a sunny, wind-protected spot, so as to keep the energy consumption within bounds.

With the barbecue smoker, which I especially like using in winter, I create the heat with a combination of charcoal briquettes and wood. With the briquettes I ensure the basic level of heat I need to operate, and with the wood I create the smoke that lends the grilled foods their special flavours.

Your classic charcoal kettle grill is also well suited to winter grilling. When I'm using one, I also use briquettes for the basic heat and wood chips of various aromas for the smoked flavours.

winter equipment

In winter I prefer to use a wood or charcoal grill such as a barbecue smoker or a Monolith ceramic grill. For quick grilling I use a gas grill, preferably with a cast-iron grate, which retains heat well.

To lend individual dishes the smoky notes they need, I use pre-soaked wood chips or dried herbs on the charcoal grill. On the barbecue smoker, I achieve the smokiness with various types of hardwood such as beech, birch or wood from stone-fruit trees.

9

what you need

The top-notch quality of your ingredients, and of course, your equipment and supplies, are the foundation for successful grilling and barbecuing. It's an unwritten law that only good quality materials lead to good results.

Recent years have seen a multitude of scandals around food, and the media have certainly played a valuable role in raising consumers' awareness of how important it is to know not only where the animals we eat come from but, more importantly, how they were raised. And while we need to turn away from mass breeding, with all its negative—even catastrophic—consequences for humans and animals (not to mention nature and the environment), we also need to learn all over again that for reasons of sustainability and out of respect for nature, fruits and vegetables should be used as the seasons offer them.

No grill master need fear that doing without imported foods at any time during the year will mean standing hungry in front of an empty grill. Every season produces foods that are perfect for grilling, and particularly with the so-called old vegetables (such as beets, parsnips or parsley root) you can conjure up wonderfully aromatic grilled dishes.

But while it's important to be careful in the selection of foods to put on your grill, you also need to exercise prudence when choosing other essential materials. For instance, I only use hardwood grown in my region and I purchase it from distributors I know. When it comes to briquettes, I make sure that they're made from beechwood and contain no lignite. They need to be bonded with natural starch, not with chemical additives. It goes without saying that I don't use imported coal made from tropical woods. And we should return to using natural starters, so that our grilled foods are not subjected to offensive odours.

Of course, the equipment we grill on is also extremely important. Here, too, the rule applies: if you want to produce good quality, you need to start with good quality.

GROUND VENISON

Roast Beef

VEAL CHOP

Wild Boar Filet

Char

grill safety

- ★ Always position the grill on a secure surface.
- ★ Ensure that the grill area is a safe distance from flammable materials.
- ★ Never leave the grill unattended, and make sure that no children play in the grill area.
- ★ Never light charcoal with alcohol or gasoline—flare ups can occur.
- ★ Never pour additional liquid flammables onto already glowing charcoal.
- ★ Never extinguish burning fat or a burning grill with water; instead, smother with a fire blanket or use a powder fire extinguisher.
- ★ Burns should be treated with cold water immediately and for an extended period of time.
- ★ Do not dispose of coals and ashes until they have completely cooled down. Always have a fire blanket and powder fire extinguisher within easy reach.
- ★ Wear sturdy, closed footwear.

helpful tips

There are two distinct methods of grilling: indirect and direct. The heat source for indirect grilling is to the side of the foods to be grilled; for direct grilling, it's underneath. I particularly enjoy working with indirect heat, because it allows me to prepare the food in the gentlest way possible. Of course, this method is very time consuming, and inexperienced grill masters may find themselves in dire straits as eagerly expectant guests line up with quietly rumbling stomachs.

I, too, had to learn that planning is an essential element of successful grilling. For me, there's almost nothing worse than hungry guests standing at the grill, plates in hand, while the food is still far from ready.

I like to tide my guests over with simple finger foods, especially at family parties; you'll find a few finger food recipes in this book. To swiftly quell the sharpest hunger pangs of the particularly "difficult" cases in my circle of family and friends—who assume that the meal will be on the table when they arrive—I always keep a few sausages at the ready. This way, even the grill master can relax and enjoy the party.

rubs and marinades

There are two types of seasoning: dry and wet rubs. I prefer dry rubs. As a rule, I first rub the foods for grilling with a high-quality canola or olive oil. But, depending on the type of meat, I also use others, such as walnut, flaxseed or safflower oils.

In a dry rub, the oil merely ensures that the spice blend adheres to the food. In a wet rub, by way of contrast, the oil not only helps it adhere but also contributes to flavouring the food.

On the other hand, classical marinating, as we know it, is a method I seldom use. Because I work with only the highest quality meats, I can't bring myself to obliterate their flavours with marinades. I want my spice blends to achieve a symbiosis with the grilled foods and to enhance the foods' own inherent flavours. Naturally, I've made sure that the theme of winter is instantly recognizable in these recipes.

In the recipes I've collected for this book, I often use one of my favourite herbs. Frequently, it's oregano **(ORIGANUM VULGARE)**, also known as wild marjoram. If you want to gather it in the wild, keep an eye out for it on slopes with southern exposure, along railroad embankments, on the edges of forests and in limy or gravelly soils. Oregano is an appetite and metabolism stimulant, and has antispasmodic and diuretic properties. You can use it for dishes with game and in wild herb salt in the same way you'd use marjoram, but it has a sharper, stronger flavour. And it possesses magical qualities: oregano is used in all cleansing rituals and some incense mixtures, and is often hung in homes by the bunch.

Another herb I use in some of my winter recipes is mugwort **(ARTEMISIA VULGARIS)**. If you want to harvest it yourself, look for it along railroad embankments and in meadows. Like oregano, it's an appetite stimulant, and because it promotes digestion, it's especially well suited to seasoning fatty meats such as pork, duck or goose. Mugwort is also a tasty ingredient in wild herb salt. Magical properties have been ascribed to it as well. For First Nations peoples, it's a significant medicinal herb and accompanies them during birth and death, as they cross over between worlds.

stocking up for winter

Our ancestors showed us how to do it, and to a certain extent we, too, should use the summer and autumn months to lay in supplies of herbs and fruits for the winter. Of course, nowadays it's easy to get everything from the supermarket around the corner. But is the most convenient way always the best one? The one that leaves you with a really good feeling? Not for me.

Whenever I can, I leave the house early on Sunday morning to take a long stroll. The Rhine valley, where I live, is home to an almost inexhaustible variety of wild herbs that anyone can simply pick and dry. So on Sundays I spend a few peaceful hours out in nature, collecting mugwort, wild mint, wild oregano and other wild herbs, which I then dry in a cool, well-ventilated room. This is how I inject a little wilderness into my recipes. And naturally, there are extremely positive health benefits to using wild herbs in grilling and barbecuing.

From time to time, when hiking with my family in the mountains of Vorarlberg, I look for wild thyme, which I then infuse warm honey with for a time; this gives me wild thyme honey, both a seasoning and a cure for the winter.

I also take the opportunity to gather grass with wild herbs from meadows that haven't been fertilized with liquid manure. I then take the grass home, let it dry, and use this mountain herb hay for winter grilling.

There's plenty of specialized literature on wild herbs to help us recognize the right ones, and to provide us with information on their medicinal properties and tips on how to process them.

Of course, when collecting herbs, we need to keep in mind the following rules:

- Gather only herbs that you recognize.
- Don't collect herbs along roads or dog-walking paths.
- And, of course, be fair to nature and don't take everything from just one spot.

Salt is found in almost every spice blend—but that's not the only reason to use the best quality available.

When grilling, I use exclusively "good" salt, that is, salt that hasn't been industrially processed and to which no flavourings, anticaking agents or chemicals have been added. I prefer to use rock salt, Himalayan salt, Fleur de Sel, Murray River Salt (from Australia), black Hawaiian salt or Croatian sea salt (that my brother brings back for me from his holidays).

my spice blends

Red Seasoning Salt

I like to keep a ready supply of this red seasoning salt, which I use as the basis for other seasonings. This is my all-purpose, standard rub for all grilled meat recipes. Thoroughly combine equal parts:

    salt
    curry powder (however hot you like it)
    paprika (regular, smoked [pimentón] or hot, whatever you prefer)

Poultry Rub

Combine thoroughly:

    6 Tbsp (90 mL) red seasoning salt
    1 Tbsp (15 mL) ground dried rosemary
    1 tsp (5 mL) garlic powder
    1 Tbsp (15 mL) ground dried summer savory

Rub for Red Meats

Combine thoroughly:

    6 Tbsp (90 mL) red seasoning salt
    2 tsp (10 mL) mustard powder
    1 Tbsp (15 mL) brown sugar
    1 Tbsp (15 mL) ground cumin
    1 tsp (5 mL) chili powder
    1 tsp (5 mL) garlic powder

Fish Rub

For a fruity-exotic fish seasoning that works equally well for freshwater and saltwater fish, thoroughly combine equal parts:

    salt
    ground celery seed
    ground fenugreek
    ground dried orange peel
    ground black pepper
    ground white pepper
    ground cardamom
    ground dried medium-hot chili peppers

Game Rub

Combine thoroughly:

    6 Tbsp (90 mL) red seasoning salt
    2 tsp (10 mL) ground dried oregano
    2 tsp (10 mL) ground dried rosemary
    1 tsp (5 mL) ground cardamom
    1/2 tsp (2 mL) ground anise seed
    1 tsp (5 mL) crushed pink peppercorn
    1 tsp (5 mL) ground juniper berries
    1 tsp (5 mL) ground bay leaves
    2 tsp (10 mL) garam masala

Wild Herb Salt

    4 cups (1 L) coarse-grained moist sea salt
    1 Tbsp (15 mL) fresh oregano, finely chopped
    1 Tbsp (15 mL) fresh wild thyme, finely chopped
    1 Tbsp (15 mL) fresh wild mint, finely chopped
    1 Tbsp (15 mL) fresh mugwort leaves and seeds, finely chopped
    1 Tbsp (15 mL) angelica root, finely chopped

Combine thoroughly and allow the flavours to blend for 2–3 weeks in a closed container. Then grind finely with mortar and pestle and fill into smaller containers. This is an excellent seasoning salt for game, winter vegetables, dips and sauces.

• •

Dried Fruit

Preserving fruits by drying them is becoming ever more popular. For me, dried fruits are an integral part of winter grilling, and I use them in every possible combination. I'm fortunate in that I can always get dried fruits of the highest quality from a friend, who's always eager and curious to see what I'm going to make out of them. The following dried fruits are especially well suited to winter grilling: apples, apricots, pineapples, pears, dates, figs and damson plums.

game:
a healthy delicacy

Although game is very healthy, it still plays second fiddle on most local menus. But its distinctive flavours and low fat content make it particularly well suited to the "healthy kitchen." Particularly in winter, when seasoned with wintry flavours, game dishes are a wonderful delicacy.

The animals' relatively stress-free lives in the great outdoors, their unlimited freedom of movement and their varied diets of herbs and grasses are all directly responsible for the flavour of their meat.

Along with fish, game is one of the types of meat with the highest protein content. It contains more protein than the meat of domestically raised animals. In addition, game has a very low fat content, and therefore contains less cholesterol than domestic meat. Fat acts as a flavour carrier, but this attribute can be fully developed with a fat content of as little as one or two percent.

Most butchers carry game, but you can also buy it in delicatessen stores or directly from hunters.

When you buy top-quality game from a hunter or butcher, you can be sure that the following standards have been met:
• only healthy, well-nourished game expertly killed by a hunter will be offered
• the meat will have been refrigerated very shortly after the animal's death, therefore there will be no interruption of the cooling chain
• you will get appropriate and hygienically impeccable maintenance and processing of the meat
• the retailer will adhere to the optimal maturation period for meat
• the meat will be kept in a refrigerated room that conforms to legally set standards
• the meat will be processed in rooms that conform to legally set standards

Next to salt and pepper, the best seasonings for game are fresh herbs, of which juniper, coriander, marjoram, rosemary, thyme and mugwort are the most suitable ones. But orange and lemon peel, cloves, cinnamon, ginger, lebkuchen or gingerbread spice, allspice, gin and port also lend interesting and utterly delightful flavours to game.

Recommended internal temperatures for optimal meat quality:

Wild boar roast (neck)	165–170°F (75–78°C)
Wild boar (loin)	145–150°F (62–64°C)
Wild boar (filet)	140–145°F (60–62°C)
Wild boar (leg)	160–165°F (72–75°C)
Roe deer and venison (roast)	165–170°F (75–78°C)
Roe deer and venison (leg)	150–160°F (65–72°C)
Roe deer and venison (loin), rare . .	140–145°F (60–63°C)
Wild poultry, medium rare	150–160°F (65–70°C)
Hare (saddle)	130–140°F (55–60°C)

recipes

FINGERFOOD

Finger food is the perfect start to any grill party. Together with a glass of wine or beer—or in winter, hot mulled wine—it can put your guests in the mood for a fantastic feast. In winter I naturally grill finger foods that are somewhat heartier, but not without subtlety. And of course, whenever possible, I use local ingredients.

bacon-wrapped cheese cubes

INGREDIENTS:

32 slices bacon

sixteen 3/4-inch (2 cm) cubes full-flavoured, firm cheese (a mountain cheese such as Emmenthal or Gruyère, ripened for 8 months)

2 Tbsp (30 mL) honey

2 Tbsp (30 mL) dried thyme

Lay half of the bacon slices out on a board. Place a cheese cube on each slice, season with some honey and thyme, and wrap the bacon slices around the cheese cubes. Then wrap the remaining bacon slices around the open sides of the cubes to make closed packages out of which the melted cheese can't easily escape.

Grill the cubes from all sides over direct heat on a very hot grill until the bacon is crispy.

lebkuchen with bacon and chili

INGREDIENTS:

16 slices bacon

sixteen 3/4-inch (2 cm) cubes lebkuchen
or gingerbread

16 thin strips hot chili pepper

2 Tbsp (30 mL) honey

Lay bacon slices out on a board. Place 1 lebkuchen or
gingerbread cube and 1 chili pepper slice on each, then
season with a drop of honey. Roll up and grill over very hot
direct heat until bacon is crispy.

Vegetarians are unfortunately somewhat at a disadvantage when it comes to grilling, because it's usually all about meat. Most times, they're downright fobbed off with grilled cheese or some indifferently prepared tofu product. But Mother Nature also offers us fabulous vegetables in winter, and all we really need to do is discover them and try them out. There's a vegetarian in my family, and I always grill separately for her.

grilled winter vegetables

Spread vegetables out in a large aluminum roasting pan and drizzle with olive oil. Season with oregano and rosemary. Mix carefully, then grill over direct heat at about 480°F (250°C) until vegetables are al dente. Arrange on a platter and season to taste with salt, orange zest and Szechuan pepper. Drizzle with olive oil and serve with homemade bread.

INGREDIENTS:

2 yellow carrots, peeled and cut lengthwise into 8 pieces

2 parsnips, peeled and cut lengthwise into 8 pieces

4 king oyster mushrooms, cut into 1/2-inch (1 cm) thick slices

2 small fennel bulbs, cut in half

2 Spanish onions, cut in half

1 kohlrabi, peeled and cut into 1/2-inch (1 cm) thick slices

5 Tbsp (75 mL) olive oil

1 tsp (5 mL) finely chopped fresh oregano

1 tsp (5 mL) finely chopped fresh rosemary

2 tsp (10 mL) salt

1–2 tsp (5–10 mL) orange zest

Szechuan pepper, to taste

INGREDIENTS:

10 prunes (approx.)

6 Tbsp (90 mL) plum jam

4 tsp (20 mL) plum brandy

chili powder, to taste

2 ripe camembert cheese in
wooden containers

YOU'LL ALSO NEED:

1 cedar plank, pre-soaked in
water for at least 5 hours

kitchen string

winter camembert

Cut prunes into thin strips. In a bowl, mix with jam and brandy, season
to taste with chili powder and let stand about 1 hour for the flavours
to blend.

Place camemberts (if possible, with bottom parts of their containers)
on the plank. If needed, tie kitchen string around the containers so that
they don't come apart during grilling. Spread plum mixture evenly over
camemberts.

Using indirect heat, grill with lid closed at about 400°F (200°C) until
cheese begins to melt (this takes about 10 to 15 minutes). Serve with
toasted white bread.

Combine honey, mustard, and chili. Season salmon on flesh side with fish rub, then coat with honey-mustard-chili mixture. Let sit about 10 minutes for salmon to absorb seasonings. Using indirect heat, grill on plank for 30 minutes at about 250–275°F (120–140°C).

salmon

INGREDIENTS:

2 Tbsp (30 mL) honey
2 Tbsp (30 mL) sweet whole-grain mustard
1/2 tsp (2 mL) chili
1 whole salmon fillet, ready for grilling
2 tsp (10 mL) Fish Rub (page 23)

YOU'LL ALSO NEED:

1–2 cedar planks, soaked in water for about 5 hours

Fish fillets can be smoked on practically any grill: on a gas grill with a smoke box (ask your specialty dealer), on a kettle barbecue or water smoker with pre-soaked wood chips, and, of course, on a barbecue smoker with wood. In this recipe, I smoke the side dish as well. This makes for a tasty dish, and you can vary the level of smokiness.

Brush flesh side of fillets with some olive oil. For the rub, combine ingredients thoroughly. Season oiled side of fillets liberally.

Mix mushrooms and chili peppers with remaining olive oil and sprinkle with salt and rosemary. Pierce stems of mushrooms and chili peppers with skewer, then thread kitchen string through holes. Hang vegetables up in smoker tower.

Arrange trout fillets on smoke tower grate and smoke at 175°F (80°C) for about 50–60 minutes. Finely slice mushrooms and chili peppers. Season fish with dill and arrange on vegetables. Enjoy with a robust white wine such as a Barrique Chardonnay.

smoked trout fillets with smoked mushrooms and habaneros

INGREDIENTS:

4 trout fillets, skin on

1/4 cup (60 mL) olive oil, divided

rub (see below)

6 porcini mushrooms

4–6 chili peppers (habanero or, if you prefer, a milder type)

1 tsp (5 mL) salt

2 tsp (10 mL) chopped fresh rosemary

4 tsp (20 mL) fresh dill, finely chopped

YOU'LL ALSO NEED:

kitchen string

RUB:

1/2 tsp (2 mL) ground fenugreek

1/2 tsp (2 mL) ground dried orange peel

1/2 tsp (2 mL) ground black pepper

1/2 tsp (2 mL) ground white pepper

1/2 tsp (2 mL) ground celery seed

1/2 tsp (2 mL) ground cardamom

1/2 tsp (2 mL) medium-hot chili powder

INGREDIENTS:

2 tsp (10 mL) salt, divided

1 whole char (about 10 oz [300 g] per person)
ready for grilling

juice of 1 lemon

a few small sprigs fresh thyme

1 large Savoy cabbage

YOU'LL ALSO NEED:

kitchen string

char wrapped in savoy cabbage

Salt inside cavity of char well, and sprinkle with lemon juice; insert thyme.
Remove leaves from cabbage and wrap in 2 layers around fish. Tie with kitchen
string. Grill over direct heat with lid closed at about 350°F (180°C), about
15 minutes per side. Remove outer, burned cabbage layer, then remove skin
from fish on one side. Salt to taste and serve. The cabbage can be eaten
as a side dish.

Char is a popular fish that is ideally suited to grilling because of its somewhat higher fat content. However, make sure to use only medium-large fish; otherwise, it'll simply be too fatty. Combined with cabbage, this makes for a very interesting dish.

In a freezer bag, mix spice blend, lemon, garlic, salt and sugar with enough water to make a sauce. Marinate the chicken breasts in the liquid for about 3 hours. Pat meat dry, season with spice blend, and, using indirect heat, grill on plank at about 350°F (180°C). Brush frequently with marinade. When meat has reached an internal temperature of 150°F (67°C), let rest for 5 minutes, wrapped in foil, before serving.

RECIPE NOTE: Marinade and spice blend should be enough for 4 individual servings of chicken.

appenzell herb chicken

INGREDIENTS PER PERSON:

1 Tbsp (15 mL) spice blend (see below)

1 lemon, sliced

2 cloves garlic, sliced

2 Tbsp (30 mL) salt

1 Tbsp (15 mL) sugar

1 1/4 cups (310 mL) water (approx.)

1/2 chicken breast

marinade (see below)

MARINADE:

7 Tbsp (105 mL) apple juice

2 Tbsp (30 mL) Appenzeller Alpenbitter

2 Tbsp (30 mL) honey

2 tsp (10 mL) spice blend

SPICE BLEND:

3 Tbsp (45 mL) paprika

1 Tbsp (15 mL) garlic powder

3 Tbsp (45 mL) curry powder

1 Tbsp (15 mL) salt

1 Tbsp (15 mL) ground dried rosemary

1 Tbsp (15 mL) ground dried summer savory

YOU'LL ALSO NEED:

2 planks, pre-soaked in water for at least 5 hours

Appenzell Herb Chicken is one of my favourite recipes. This is probably because I particularly enjoy drinking Appenzeller Alpenbitter, a bitter liqueur from neighbouring Switzerland made from 42 herbs, and of course, because I also scored a win with this recipe at the World Barbecue Championship in Gronau, Germany.

Beer-can chicken is certain to be an eye-catcher at any barbecue (although in this picture it's a duck sitting on the beer can; for the recipe, see page 68). But there's another way to prepare chicken that's just as spectacular and is doable on practically any commonly used grill, provided that it can be set up for indirect grilling and has a cover.

chicken with hay

Thoroughly combine herbs and spices. Soak the herb hay for about 2 hours in the water and whisky. Stuff the chicken with the softened hay, season outside of chicken liberally with spice blend, and, using indirect heat, grill at 400°F (200°C) for 1 1/2 hours.

INGREDIENTS:
1 Tbsp (15 mL) mild smoked paprika
1 tsp (5 mL) garlic powder
1 Tbsp (15 mL) curry powder
1 tsp (5 mL) salt
1/2 tsp (2 mL) chili powder
1 tsp (5 mL) brown sugar
1 tsp (5 mL) ground cumin
1 tsp (5 mL) ground cinnamon
mountain herb hay, self-harvested or from a garden centre
about 4 cups (1 L) water
5 Tbsp + 1 tsp (80 mL) whisky or good rum
1 chicken, ready for grilling

THIS IS ALSO DELICIOUS

These two variations on the Chicken with Hay recipe are certainly worth a try. The first recipe on page 51 is quite similar to the original version but slightly more rustic in its execution and intended for those who can't quite warm to the idea of chicken combined with whisky or rum. The second one is no less interesting and could become a real eye-catcher at your grill party.

chicken with herb hay, sweet wine and cinnamon

Thoroughly combine spices. Soak herb hay for about 2 hours in sweet wine and enough water to cover hay. Stuff chicken with softened hay and cinnamon sticks, season outside of chicken liberally with spice blend and, using indirect heat, grill at 400°F (200°C) for 1 1/2 hours.

INGREDIENTS:

1 Tbsp (15 mL) mild smoked paprika

1 tsp (5 mL) garlic powder

1 Tbsp (15 mL) curry powder

1 tsp (5 mL) salt

1/2 tsp (2 mL) chili powder

1 tsp (5 mL) brown sugar

1 tsp (5 mL) ground star anise

mountain herb hay, self-harvested or from a garden centre

7 Tbsp (105 mL) sweet wine (dessert wine, ice wine, or Moscato)

1 chicken, ready for grilling

4 sticks cinnamon

chicken with oranges and cloves

INGREDIENTS:

1 Tbsp (15 mL) mild allspice

1 tsp (5 mL) garlic powder

1 Tbsp (15 mL) curry powder

1 tsp (5 mL) salt

1/2 tsp (2 mL) chili powder

1 tsp (5 mL) brown sugar

1 tsp (5 mL) ground dried orange zest

2 medium-sized oranges

20 whole cloves

1 chicken, ready for grilling

YOU'LL ALSO NEED:

2 bamboo skewers, soaked

Thoroughly combine spices, sugar and dried orange zest. Stud oranges with cloves and press down lightly to release juice. Stuff chicken with oranges, and use one skewer apiece to close cavity opening and neck cavity.

Season outside of chicken liberally with spice blend and, using indirect heat, grill at 400°F (200°C) for 1 1/2 hours.

INGREDIENTS FOR THE BRINE:

6 Tbsp (90 mL) salt

1/4 cup (60 mL) sweet paprika

1/4 cup (60 mL) curry powder

1/4 cup (60 mL) ground dried
summer savory

2 oranges, sliced

4 cloves garlic, lightly crushed

4 slices fresh ginger

6 bay leaves (dried)

5 Tbsp (75 mL) Irish whisky

INGREDIENTS FOR THE TURKEY:

1 Tbsp (15 mL) ground dried
summer savory

1 Tbsp (15 mL) ground dried rosemary

1 tsp (5 mL) ground cinnamon

3 Tbsp (45 mL) paprika

3 Tbsp (45 mL) mild curry powder

1 tsp (5 mL) ground cloves

1/2 tsp (2 mL) chili powder

1 Tbsp (15 mL) lemon pepper

1 Tbsp (15 mL) brown sugar

2 Tbsp (30 mL) salt

one 11 lb (5 kg) turkey

1/4 cup (60 mL) olive oil

YOU WILL ALSO NEED:

2 handfuls apple wood chips, pre-soaked
in water for at least 2 hours

apple juice in a spray bottle

turkey tom's way

Add all ingredients for the brine in a container large enough to hold the turkey. Stir thoroughly and add turkey. Add enough water to cover the turkey completely. Let rest overnight in fridge.

Thoroughly combine herbs, spices, brown sugar and salt. First rub turkey with oil, then rub liberally with spice blend. Preheat barbecue smoker to 250°F (120°C). Using indirect heat, grill turkey to an internal temperature of 175°F (80°C). Measure temperature on inside of leg. During grilling, smoke frequently with wood chips and spray with apple juice for a crispy skin.

I serve this with Root Vegetable Coleslaw (page 67), Potato-Apple-Pear Gratin (page 101) and, of course, a glass of good red wine. This recipe can also be prepared using a water smoker or a larger kettle grill.

On Christmas Day, when we invite my entire extended family for a meal, we serve turkey done in the barbecue smoker, a fairly untypical dish for our region. Preparations begin the day before. I brine the bird in a water-spice mix for 24 hours to flavour the meat—from the inside—of our festive repast's main protagonist.

stuffed beets

INGREDIENTS PER PERSON:

3 1/2 oz (100 g) Montafon Sura Kees
or feta cheese

2 cloves garlic, finely chopped

2 Tbsp (30 mL) grated walnuts

1 Tbsp olive oil

1 tsp (5 mL) oregano

1 cooked beet

Combine cheese, garlic, walnuts, oil and oregano to make a paste. Hollow out beets and fill with mixture. Using indirect heat, grill at 400°F (200°C) until cheese melts, about 20 to 30 minutes.

turkey for a smaller crowd

INGREDIENTS:

1 Tbsp (15 mL) ground dried summer savory

1 Tbsp (15 mL) ground dried rosemary

3 Tbsp (45 mL) paprika

3 Tbsp (45 mL) mild curry powder

1 tsp (5 mL) ground cinnamon

1 tsp (5 mL) ground cloves

1/2 tsp (2 mL) chili powder

1 Tbsp (15 mL) lemon pepper

1 Tbsp (15 mL) fine brown sugar

2 Tbsp (30 mL) salt

one 3 lb (1.5 kg) turkey drumstick

1/4 cup (60 mL) olive oil

3 Tbsp (45 mL) rice syrup

YOU'LL ALSO NEED:

apple juice in a spray bottle

1 handful pre-soaked wood chips

Thoroughly combine herbs, spices, sugar and salt. First rub turkey leg with oil, then rub liberally with spice blend. Preheat barbecue smoker or grill to 250°F (120°C). Using indirect heat, grill leg to an internal temperature of 175°F (80°C). While grilling, smoke frequently with wood chips and spray with apple juice.

Shortly before serving, brush with rice syrup, and increase temperature to 400°F (200°C) for 10 minutes, for a truly crispy skin.

This is delicious served with Root Vegetable Coleslaw (page 67) and either red wine or a robust white wine.

This is an easy variation of a dish that seems difficult at first glance. With creamed cabbage as a side dish, you're sure to score points with this wintry meal.

barbary duck breast with creamed cabbage

Combine soy sauce, ginger, honey and cinnamon to make the marinade. Score the fat layer of the duck breasts in a diamond pattern, taking care not to cut into the meat. Season the meat on all sides with paprikas, salt and pepper. Place the breasts fat side down on the grill and, using indirect heat, cook at 175°F (80°C) for about 45 minutes. (For an alternative version, use pre-soaked wood chips.) Turn meat, brush fat side with marinade, and grill over direct heat with lid closed at about 350°F (180°C) for 10 minutes.

Finely slice cabbage. In a cast-iron pan, fry speck and onion until browned. Add cabbage and deglaze with cream. Cook for about 10 minutues, then season to taste with salt and smoked paprika. Thinly slice duck breast and serve on creamed cabbage.

INGREDIENTS:
marinade (see below)
1 small duck breast
1 tsp (5 mL) smoked paprika
1 tsp (5 mL) sweet paprika
1 tsp (5 mL) salt
1 tsp (5 mL) ground black pepper
1 head cabbage
1/4 cup (60 mL) speck
1 onion, finely chopped
3 cups (750 mL) whipping cream

FOR THE MARINADE:
2 Tbsp (30 mL) soy sauce
1 tsp (5 mL) ground ginger
2 Tbsp (30 mL) honey
2 tsp (10 mL) ground cinnamon

Here's a different, Austrian take on the American classic of the barbecue world, made with winter root vegetables.

root vegetable coleslaw

INGREDIENTS:
1 celeriac, grated
2 orange carrots, grated
1 yellow carrot, grated
1 onion, thinly sliced
1/4 cup (60 mL) mayonnaise
1 cup (250 mL) sour cream
2 Tbsp (30 mL) oil
2 Tbsp (30 mL) apple cider vinegar
1 tsp (5 mL) salt
1 tsp (5 mL) crushed peppercorns
fresh horseradish, grated (optional)

Combine vegetables with remaining ingredients and mix thoroughly. Let sit overnight in fridge to blend flavours. Before serving, season to taste with salt and pepper and, if desired, grated horseradish.

This recipe is based on the well-known and much-loved dish Beer-Can Chicken. I think the idea of the beer can is genius, and the red wine in this rather more elegant variation with wild duck lends the dish a distinguished note.

beer-can duck

Combine poultry rub, mugwort and harissa. Zest one orange. Set aside zest and squeeze juice from 1 orange. Rub outside of duck first with juice, then with spice mixture. Fill can with wine and zest and insert into cavity of duck. Using indirect heat, grill with lid closed at about 400°F (200°C) for about 1 hour.

Peel and slice the other orange, and toss slices in butter. Salt to taste and serve with carved duck.

INGREDIENTS:

2 Tbsp (30 mL) Poultry Rub (page 23)

1/2 tsp (2 mL) ground dried mugwort

1 tsp (5 mL) dry harissa

2 oranges, divided

one 2 lb (1 kg) wild duck, ready for grilling

1 empty beer or soft drink can

1 cup (250 mL) red wine (Merlot, Blauer Zweigelt or Cabernet Sauvignon)

2 Tbsp (30 mL) butter

1/2 tsp (2 mL) salt

INGREDIENTS:

2 eggs

7 Tbsp (105 mL) milk

5 Tbsp (75 mL) knodelbrot or small croutons

6 chestnuts, cooked

1 tsp (5 mL) salt

pepper, to taste

2 Tbsp (30 mL) Poultry Rub (page 23)

1/2 tsp (2 mL) ground dried mugwort

1 tsp (5 mL) dry harissa

1 orange

one 2 lb (1 kg) wild duck, ready for grilling

YOU'LL ALSO NEED:

1 bamboo skewer, soaked

stuffed wild duck

For the stuffing, whisk eggs and mix well with milk, bread cubes and chestnuts. Season to taste with salt and pepper.

Combine Poultry Rub, mugwort and harissa. Squeeze juice from orange. Rub outside of duck first with juice, then with spice mixture. Fill stuffing into cavity of duck; seal with skewer. Using indirect heat, grill with lid closed at about 400°F (200°C) for about 1 hour.

Practically every grill master is judged by his or her ribs, and that's why there's such an enormous diversity of recipes. Especially when it comes to spare ribs, there are no limits to where your imagination can take you. I hope that these three versions of my spare ribs will inspire you.

Here too, I prefer a dry rub. No matter how I season the ribs or refine them after grilling, there's one thing I do for all versions: I remove the membrane and marinate the ribs for two to three hours, flesh-side down, in apple juice to which I've added a dash of apple cider vinegar.

Marinating the ribs this way tenderizes the ribs and has a positive effect on the subsequent grilling. These rib recipes are suitable for smokers, kettle grills and all gas grills.

INGREDIENTS:
marinade (see below)
4 racks spare ribs, membrane removed
spice blend, divided (see below)
7 Tbsp (105 mL) apple juice
glaze (see below)

MARINADE:
one 3/4 cup (435 mL) apple juice (approx.)
2 Tbsp (30 mL) apple cider vinegar

SPICE BLEND:
1 tsp (5 mL) ground cumin
1 tsp (5 mL) ground dried roasted onions or onion flakes
1 tsp (5 mL) garlic powder
1 tsp (5 mL) salt
1 tsp (5 mL) pepper
2 tsp (10 mL) paprika
2 tsp (10 mL) curry powder
1/2 tsp (2 mL) chili powder
2 tsp (10 mL) brown sugar
1 tsp (5 mL) garam masala

GLAZE:
3 Tbsp (45 mL) honey
1 tsp (5 mL) ginger, freshly grated
1 tsp (5 mL) garlic, finely chopped
2 Tbsp (30 mL) soy sauce
1/4 cup (60 mL) apple juice

YOU'LL ALSO NEED:
aluminum foil
plastic wrap

wintry spare ribs

Marinate ribs for 2–3 hours.

Thoroughly combine rub ingredients, then liberally season ribs with spice blend. Set remaining spice blend aside. Wrap ribs in plastic wrap and refrigerate for 2–3 hours for ribs to absorb seasonings.

Over direct heat, grill flesh side of ribs at a high temperature, then wrap together with 7 Tbsp (105 mL) apple juice in aluminum foil, flesh side up. Using indirect heat, grill with lid closed at 250°F (120°C) for 2 hours.

Meanwhile, for the glaze, combine ginger, garlic, honey, apple juice, soy sauce and the remaining spice blend.

Open foil and brush flesh side with glaze. Increase grill temperature to about 400°F (200°C) and, with lid closed, glaze ribs for about 10 minutes.

herb spare ribs

Marinate ribs for 2–3 hours.

Thoroughly combine rub ingredients, then liberally season damp ribs with rub. Set remaining rub aside. Wrap ribs in plastic wrap and refrigerate for 2–3 hours for ribs to absorb seasonings.

Over direct heat, grill flesh side of ribs at a high temperature, then wrap together with 7 Tbsp (105 mL) apple juice in aluminum foil, flesh side up. Using indirect heat, grill with lid closed at 250°F (120°C) for 2 hours.

Meanwhile, for the glaze, combine ginger, garlic, honey, Appenzeller Alpenbitter, apple juice and the remaining spice blend.

Open foil and brush flesh side with glaze. Increase grill temperature to about 400°F (200°C) and, with lid closed, glaze ribs about 10 minutes.

INGREDIENTS:

marinade (see below)

4 racks spare ribs, membrane removed

rub, divided (see below)

7 Tbsp (105 mL) apple juice

glaze (see below)

MARINADE:

1 3/4 cup (435 mL) apple juice (approx.)

2 Tbsp (30 mL) apple cider vinegar

RUB:

1 tsp (5 mL) ground cumin

1 tsp (5 mL) onion powder

1 tsp (5 mL) garlic powder

1 tsp (5 mL) salt

1 tsp (5 mL) ground black pepper

2 tsp (10 mL) paprika

2 tsp (10 mL) curry powder

1/2 tsp (2 mL) chili powder

1 tsp (5 mL) brown sugar

1/2 tsp (2 mL) ground allspice

GLAZE:

1 tsp (5 mL) freshly grated ginger

1 tsp (5 mL) finely chopped garlic

3 Tbsp (45 mL) honey

1/4 cup (60 mL) Appenzeller Alpenbitter

1/4 cup (60 mL) apple juice

YOU'LL ALSO NEED:

aluminum foil

plastic wrap

INGREDIENTS:

marinade (see below)

4 racks spare ribs, membrane removed

rub, divided (see below)

7 Tbsp (105 mL) apple juice

glaze (see below)

MARINADE:

1 3/4 cup (435 mL) apple juice (approx.)

2 Tbsp (30 mL) apple cider vinegar

RUB:

1/2 tsp (2 mL) ground cinnamon

1 tsp (5 mL) ground celery seed

1 tsp (5 mL) smoked salt

1 tsp (5 mL) ground black pepper

2 tsp (10 mL) smoked paprika

2 tsp (10 mL) curry powder

1/2 tsp (2 mL) hot chili powder

1 tsp (5 mL) brown sugar

1/2 tsp (2 mL) ground cloves

1/2 tsp (2 mL) ground caraway seed

1/2 tsp (2 mL) ground dried orange peel

GLAZE:

1/4 cup (60 mL) orange marmalade

1 tsp (5 mL) finely chopped garlic

1/4 cup (60 mL) soy sauce

1/4 cup (60 mL) orange juice

YOU'LL ALSO NEED:

aluminum foil

plastic wrap

tom's winter ribs

Marinate ribs for 2–3 hours.

Thoroughly combine rub ingredients, then liberally season ribs with rub. Set remaining rub aside. Wrap ribs in plastic wrap and refrigerate for 2–3 hours for ribs to absorb seasonings.

Over direct heat, grill flesh side of ribs at a high temperature, then wrap together with 7 Tbsp (105 mL) apple juice in aluminum foil, flesh side up. Using indirect heat, grill with lid closed at 250°F (120°C) for 2 hours.

Meanwhile, for the glaze, combine marmalade, garlic, soy sauce, orange juice and the remaining rub.

Open foil and brush flesh side with glaze. Increase grill temperature to about 400°F (200°C) and, with lid closed, glaze ribs about 10 minutes.

A truly princely dish for the cold winter months. Easy to prepare, but a sure-fire hit with your guests.

studded pork loin

INGREDIENTS:
one 2 lb (1 kg) pork loin,
with a layer of fat
20 slivers of garlic
several sprigs fresh rosemary
10 bay leaves, soaked in water
2 tsp (10 mL) salt
2 tsp (10 mL) ground caraway seed
2 tsp (10 mL) ground cloves

YOU WILL ALSO NEED:
eisbock or bock beer in a spray bottle

With a sharp knife, score sheath of fat in a diamond pattern, taking care not to cut into meat. With a pointed knife, make a small hole in the centre of each fat diamond. Insert 1 garlic sliver and a few rosemary needles in each hole. Distribute bay leaves evenly in grooves in between.

Season meat on all sides with salt, caraway and cloves. Refrigerate overnight for seasonings to be absorbed. Using indirect heat, grill at 195–250°F (90–120°C) to an internal temperature of 150°F (65°C), spraying frequently with beer.

Blood sausage eaten cold, known in eastern Austria as "Blunze," is an old specialty that's almost fallen into oblivion. It's enjoyed as a snack, served with plenty of horseradish and sourdough bread. This version, grilled and combined with apples, makes an excellent hors d'oeuvre.

INGREDIENTS:

16 slices tart baking apple

twelve 1/2 inch (1 cm)-thick slices blood sausage

2 Tbsp (30 mL) horseradish, freshly grated

2 tsp (10 mL) salt, divided

1 tsp (5 mL) pepper, divided

4 tsp (20 mL) orange zest

1 cup (250 mL) sour cream

apple–blood sausage lasagna with horseradish

Grill apple and sausage slices on both sides over direct heat (about 400°F [200°C]) until apples are soft and sausage has taken on a bit of colour. Season apples with salt and pepper; season sausage with orange zest.

Starting with an apple slice and alternating, stack 4 apple slices and 3 sausage slices. Repeat to make 4 stacks in all. Combine horseradish and sour cream, season to taste with salt and pepper, and serve with stacks.

Serve with toasted sourdough bread.

sliders with curry-mustard sauce

INGREDIENTS:

1 lb (500 g) ground beef (20% fat content) from a reliable butcher

1 Tbsp (15 mL) Worcestershire sauce

2 tsp (10 mL) salt (plus extra for post-grill seasoning, to taste)

1 tsp (5 mL) pepper (plus extra for post-grill seasoning, to taste)

6 Tbsp (90 mL) mustard

3 dill pickles, finely chopped

1 Tbsp (15 mL) curry powder

8 slider buns

2 handfuls lamb's lettuce

YOU WILL ALSO NEED:

aluminum foil

Combine ground beef with Worcestershire sauce and season with salt and pepper. Shape the meat into 8 patties about 5/8 inch (1 1/2 cm) high and grill over direct heat about 3–4 minutes per side. Let sit in a warm place about 3–4 minutes, covered with aluminum foil. Combine mustard, pickles and curry powder, and season with salt and pepper. Serve sliders in buns with curry mustard and lamb's lettuce.

This somewhat rustic side dish from the grill may not win your heart at first glance. But the uncomplicated barbecue sauce and the subtle wild herbs combine to produce a flavour that will truly tickle your taste buds.

grilled cabbage

In a pan, lightly brown bacon and onion 3–5 minutes. Remove from heat and add all remaining ingredients except for the cabbage.

Core cabbage, cutting generously. Place cabbage on grill with opening topmost and fill with bacon-onion mixture. Using indirect heat and wood chips, grill on a kettle barbecue at 350°F (180°C) for about 1–1 1/2 hours.

INGREDIENTS:

4 thick slices bacon, diced

1 small onion, finely chopped

1/4 cup (60 mL) barbecue sauce

2 tsp (10 mL) fresh oregano, finely chopped

2 tsp (10 mL) fresh rosemary, finely chopped

2 tsp (10 mL) salt

1 tsp (5 mL) pepper

1 tsp (5 mL) orange zest

1 medium-sized (white) cabbage

YOU WILL ALSO NEED:

1 handtul apple wood chips, pre-soaked in water

One of my favourite foods and an absolute classic of Austrian cuisine is Tafelspitz, or boiled beef. I've thought long and hard about how to prepare this wonderful dish on a barbecue smoker or grill.

Veal Tafelspitz is particularly delicious. The important thing with this cut of meat, which is actually meant for braising, is that it be cooked at a relatively low temperature (210–250°F [100–120°C]). And when the veal is brought to the right internal temperature, and served with this unusual side dish, it turns out to be a true culinary delight.

veal tafelspitz with apple-horseradish vegetables

INGREDIENTS:
1 1/2 tsp (2 mL) salt, divided
1/4 tsp (1 mL) ground allspice
1/4 tsp (1 mL) ground caraway seed
1 tsp (5 mL) sweet paprika
1/2 tsp (2 mL) curry powder
1/2 tsp (2 mL) ground dried thyme
2 lb (1 kg) veal top round
6 tart baking apples
2 Tbsp (30 mL) olive oil
pepper, to taste
2 Tbsp (30 mL) fresh horseradish, grated

YOU WILL ALSO NEED:
freshly pressed apple juice in a spray bottle

Combine 1/2 tsp salt with the allspice, caraway seed, paprika, curry powder and thyme. Season meat liberally on all sides.

Smoke meat in smoker at 250°F (120°C) for a maximum of about 1 1/2 hours (or using indirect heat, grill on another type of grill), until meat has reached an internal temperature of 150°F (65°C). Spray frequently with apple juice to prevent meat from drying out.

Core apples and cut into evenly sized 3/4-inch (2 cm) cubes.

Heat oil in cast-iron pan or wok and fry apple pieces until soft. Season to taste with salt and pepper and mix in horseradish. Serve with meat.

The first time I made the following recipe, it almost drove me out of my mind. We had invited guests for a barbecue dinner, announcing that we'd be serving—as always—something special. I ordered beef ribs from the butcher, totally underestimating what their preparation would involve. In my euphoria, I assumed that beef ribs would need a cooking time similar to that of pork ribs. Now, I can get top-quality pork spare ribs onto the table in three hours. For the beef ribs, I needed—believe it or not—seven hours until my inner quality control could declare them ready to eat. Unfortunately, by this time all the side dishes and the dessert had already been consumed, and the ribs did not receive quite the appreciation that they (and I) actually deserved. At the next barbecue dinner with the same guests, and after palpable initial skepticism—except on my part, of course—the beef ribs were a resounding success.

barbecue smoker beef ribs

INGREDIENTS:

2 racks beef ribs, trimmed by your butcher

8 cups (2 L) apple juice

1 tsp (5 mL) ground dried rosemary

2 Tbsp (30 mL) ground cumin

2 Tbsp (30 mL) sweet paprika

1 Tbsp (15 mL) salt

1 Tbsp (15 mL) brown sugar

1 tsp (5 mL) chili powder

1/2 tsp (2 mL) ground coriander

1 tsp (5 mL) mustard powder

In a large bowl, marinate ribs in apple juice for 3 hours. Thoroughly combine herbs and spices. Remove ribs from juice, drain and rub liberally with spice blend. Set juice aside. Wrap ribs in plastic wrap and refrigerate, preferably overnight, for ribs to absorb seasonings.

Preheat barbecue or water smoker 195°F (90°C). Smoke ribs about 2 hours at 175–195°F (80–90°C). Increase temperature to 250°F (120°C) and grill ribs a further 5 hours, spraying frequently with the leftover apple juice.

INGREDIENTS PER PERSON:

1 potato

1 Tbsp (15 mL) fresh rosemary, finely chopped

2 tsp (10 mL) salt

1 tsp (5 mL) pepper

6 Tbsp (90 mL) sour cream

grated cheese, for topping

YOU WILL ALSO NEED:

an aluminum roasting pan or aluminum cups for
each potato

stuffed potatoes

Cut potatoes in half, place cut-side down in aluminum
roasting pan, cover and grill over direct heat until soft.
Using a melon baller, scoop out potatoes. Mix potato
insides with rosemary, salt, pepper and sour cream until
smooth. Fill into potato skins and top with cheese.

Using indirect heat, grill at 400°F (200°C) for about
15 minutes, until cheese is melted.

I like to serve homemade chutney as a small, elegant accompaniment, and I always make sure to combine sweet, sour and hot. It is excellent with many grilled foods, such as steak.

apple-fig chutney

INGREDIENTS:

2 Tbsp (30 mL) olive oil
1/2 onion, finely chopped
1 Tbsp (15 mL) apple cider vinegar
2 apples, cored and diced
4 dried figs, diced
1 small chili pepper, finely chopped
2 Tbsp (30 mL) apple jelly
1/2 tsp (2 mL) salt
1/2 tsp (2 mL) pepper

Heat oil in a small pot and sauté onion until transparent. Deglaze with vinegar and add remaining ingredients. Cook until reduced to preferred consistency and fill, while still hot, into clean jars. Turn jars upside down to cool.

When it comes to beef, I prefer steaks that are at least 1 1/4 inches (3 cm) thick, regardless of the breed of cattle or the cut of the meat.

The process of grilling the various beef steaks (entrecôte, rib eye, rump, sirloin, etc.) is always the same. I place the steak on the hot grate over direct heat and wait until the meat releases juices. Then I turn the meat and wait until the juices are released from that side. Then I let the meat sit in a warm place, wrapped in aluminum foil, for five minutes.

Not until then do I season with coarse sea salt and a top-quality pepper or pepper blend. This way, the meat's natural flavours can be fully enjoyed.

This dish makes a wonderful Christmas Eve treat for the ones you love.

roast beef with lebkuchen

INGREDIENTS:

spice blend, divided (see below)
6 Tbsp (90 mL) grated lebkuchen
or gingerbread
3/4 cup (185 mL) dark beer
7 Tbsp (105 mL) apple juice
7 Tbsp (105 mL) pear juice
2 lb (1 kg) lean beef

SPICE BLEND:

2 tsp (10 mL) salt
2 tsp (10 mL) mustard powder
2 tsp (10 mL) brown sugar
2 tsp (10 mL) ground cumin
1 tsp (5 mL) chili powder
1 tsp (5 mL) garlic powder
2 tsp (10 mL) paprika
1 tsp (5 mL) ground black pepper

Thoroughly combine spice blend ingredients.

Make a marinade from lebkuchen, beer, fruit juices and 2 Tbsp (30 mL) spice blend. Season beef with remaining spice blend. Using indirect heat, grill at 250°F (120°C) to an internal temperature of 135°F (58°C). Brush with marinade continuously, stopping as soon as an internal temperature of 130°F (56°C) has been reached. Before serving, let rest for a few minutes in a warm place.

Potato, Apple, and Pear Gratin (see below) goes well with this.

potato, apple and pear gratin
in a dutch oven

INGREDIENTS:

2 lb (1 kg) potatoes
3 winter apples
3 pears
2 onions
7 oz (200 g) feta cheese
1 3/4 cup (435 mL) whipping cream
2 cups (500 mL) crème fraîche
2 eggs
1 tsp (5 mL) salt
1 tsp (5 mL) pepper
1 tsp (5 mL) paprika
1 pinch grated nutmeg
1 tsp (5 mL) dried thyme
2 Tbsp (30 mL) olive oil

YOU WILL ALSO NEED:

25 briquettes

Peel potatoes and slice thinly. Peel apples and pears, core and slice thinly. Chop onions finely and crumble feta. In a bowl, whisk together cream, crème fraîche, eggs, salt and spices.

Place about 10 glowing briquettes under a Dutch oven and sauté onions in olive oil. Alternately layer potato slices, apples, pears, feta and onions in the Dutch oven. Pour sauce over layered ingredients. Cover, place 15 further briquettes on lid, and cook gratin about 1 1/2 hours.

VARIATION: Refine the gratin by adding a handful of raisins to the sauce.

lamb shoulder

Rub lamb with oil. Combine herbs, salt and pepper and use it to season meat liberally on all sides. For best results, refrigerate several hours or overnight in plastic wrap for seasonings to be absorbed.

Prepare grill for indirect grilling or preheat smoker. Grill lamb at a maximum of 250°F (120°C) to an internal temperature of 150–155°F (65–67°C). Smoke frequently during grill process.

INGREDIENTS:

1 3/4 lb (800 g) boneless lean lamb shoulder
2 Tbsp (30 mL) olive oil
1 Tbsp (15 mL) fresh rosemary, finely chopped
1 tsp (5 mL) fresh cilantro, finely chopped
1 tsp (5 mL) fresh mint, finely chopped
1 tsp (5 mL) salt
1 tsp (5 mL) pepper

YOU'LL ALSO NEED:

wood chips or a smoke box (although if you own a barbecue smoker, this would be your first choice)

wintry bread

In a bowl, combine flour, yeast, salt, olive oil and water to make a stiff dough. Let rise in a warm place until dough has doubled in volume. Knead dough again and divide into 4 equal balls. Roll out with a rolling pin and place some cheese in the middle of each piece. Grate pear over pieces. Seal dough to make buns (rolls). Using indirect heat, bake at 350–400°F (180–200°C) for 30 minutes. To test, take one bun from grill and tap bottom with your fingers. If it sounds hollow, the buns are done.

INGREDIENTS:

4 3/4 cups (1.2 L) all-purpose flour
1 package (2 1/4 tsp [11 mL]) dry yeast
1 tsp (5 mL) salt
2 Tbsp (30 mL) olive oil
1 cup (250 mL) lukewarm water
2 oz (60 g) blue cheese
1 pear

rack of lamb

Mix together salt, juniper berries, pepper, rosemary and olive oil to make a marinade. Brush mixture onto lamb and refrigerate 2–3 hours in plastic wrap for seasonings to be absorbed. Combine butter, bread crumbs, Parmesan and remaining marinade to make a bread-crumb coating. Pat lamb dry and grill flesh-side down over direct heat (400°F [200°C]) about 5 minutes. Remove from grill and brush bread-crumb coating liberally over flesh side. Using indirect heat, grill lamb at about 350°F (180°C) for a further 5 minutes.

For the side dish, brush cut sides of parsnips with olive oil and grill over direct heat (about 200°C) for about 7–8 minutes.

INGREDIENTS:

1 tsp (5 mL) salt
1 tsp (5 mL) finely crushed juniper berries
1 tsp (5 mL) pepper
1 tsp (5 mL) ground dried rosemary
1/4 cup (60 mL) olive oil, divided
2 racks of lamb, trimmed
2 Tbsp (30 mL) soft butter
2 Tbsp (30 mL) bread crumbs
1 Tbsp (15 mL) grated Parmesan cheese
2 parsnips, halved

This is how you trim a rack of lamb:

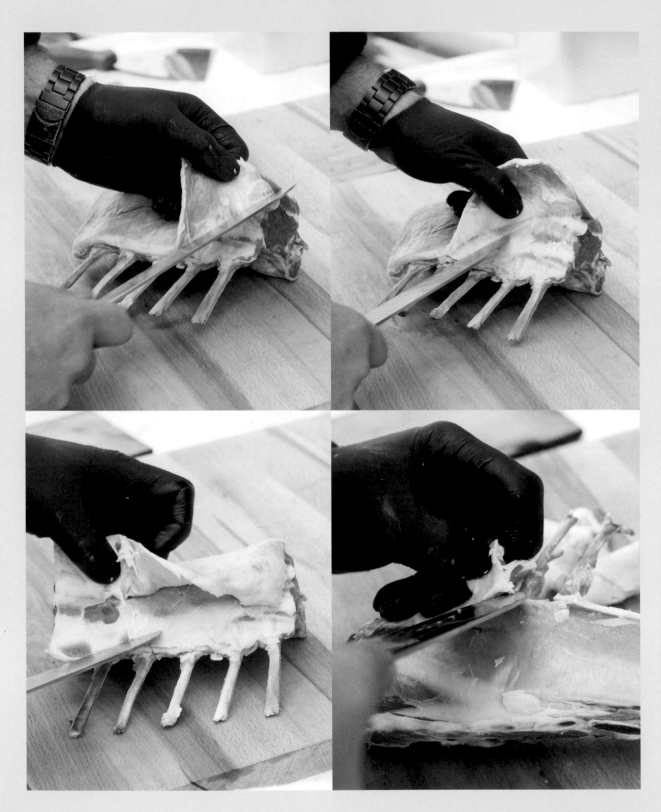

Cooking game is a challenge for any grill master. Because the meat has virtually no fat, it's crucial to pay close attention to the internal temperature. I almost never sear the prime cuts (loin or filet) but prefer to use indirect heat right from the beginning. This ensures that the prime cuts stay rare and moist, with no dry edges.

Game is one of the healthiest types of meats. The animals live on grass, herbs, and twigs; aren't fed any antibiotics; and normally experience no stress when killed because they die in seconds after a well-aimed hunter's shot.

From September on, game regularly plays a prominent role in my grill courses. Increasingly, connoisseurs prefer a juicy grilled piece of game to the more familiar, drowned-in-red-wine versions.

Weidmanns Dank (Hunter's thanks).

Rub venison with olive oil. Thoroughly combine paprika, salt, juniper berries, bay leaves, allspice and oregano. Season meat liberally with spice blend. Refrigerate for 3–4 hours for seasonings to be absorbed.

Remove from fridge 1 hour before grilling. Wrap juniper, rosemary and oregano sprigs around meat and secure with kitchen string.

Using indirect heat, slow roast at 250°F (120°C), with lid closed, on barbecue smoker or another grill type to an internal temperature of 140°F (60°C).

venison loin

INGREDIENTS:

one 2 lb (1 kg) venison loin, trimmed

2 Tbsp (30 mL) olive oil

1 tsp (5 mL) paprika

1 tsp (5 mL) salt

1 tsp (5 mL) juniper berries, finely chopped

1/2 tsp (2 mL) bay leaves, finely crushed

1 tsp (5 mL) ground allspice

1 tsp (5 mL) finely crushed oregano

2 sprigs fresh juniper

2 sprigs fresh rosemary

2 sprigs fresh oregano, with blossoms

YOU'LL ALSO NEED:

kitchen string

FOR THE FILLING:

1 1/4 lb (625 g) roe deer shoulder, deboned

2 Tbsp (30 mL) olive oil

1 tsp (5 mL) salt

1/2 tsp (2 mL) pepper

1/2 tsp (2 mL) ground juniper berries

1/2 tsp (2 mL) ground allspice

1/2 tsp (2 mL) ground dried oregano

1/2 tsp (2 mL) ground dried rosemary

4 medium-large mushrooms (e.g., king oyster or porcini)

FOR THE BUNS:

4 3/4 cups (1.2 L) all-purpose flour

1 package (2 1/4 tsp [11 mL]) dried yeast

1 tsp (5 mL) salt

2 Tbsp (30 mL) olive oil

1 cup (250 mL) lukewarm water

roe deer shoulder in bread

BUNS:

In a bowl, combine flour, yeast, salt, olive oil and water to make a stiff dough. Let rise in a warm place until dough has doubled in volume. Knead dough again and divide into 4 equal-sized buns. Using indirect heat, bake at 350–400°F (180–200°C) for 30 minutes. To test, take one bun from grill and tap bottom with your fingers. If it sounds hollow, the buns are done.

ROE DEER SHOULDER:

Rub meat with olive oil. Thoroughly combine salt, pepper, herbs and spices. Sear meat on all sides, then, using indirect heat, grill at 250–275°F (120–140°C) for about 1 hour, to an internal temperature of 160–165°F (72–74°C). Wrap meat in aluminum foil and let rest about 10 minutes in a warm place. Cut mushrooms into bite-sized pieces. In a grill pan or wok, sauté until al dente. Cut meat into small pieces and mix with mushrooms. If needed, season to taste with salt and pepper. Fill meat-mushroom mixture into buns—done!

Depending on your taste, garnish with wild cranberry jam seasoned with chili peppers and Indonesian long pepper.

Like so many of my recipes, this one grew out of a whim. My boys love to eat meat off the spit, wrapped into bread with lettuce, sliced tomatoes and onions, and yogurt sauce; in urban areas, you can find it on practically every street corner.

This rather more upscale version is a slowed-down, country-style variation— and certainly doesn't deserve the label "fast food".

Cooking saddle of hare can be a bit tricky. It's practically doomed to turn out dry, but there's a simple method to prepare it on the grill—with delicious results that keep it tender.

saddle of hare

INGREDIENTS:

12 saddles of hare, deboned
pepper, to taste
24 slices prosciutto (e.g., San Daniele or Parma)
3 porcini mushrooms, sliced
2–3 Tbsp (30–45 mL) olive oil
salt, to taste

Season hare saddles with black pepper, then wrap in prosciutto. Marinate mushrooms in olive oil and salt. Grill meat on all sides over direct heat (about 480°F [250°C]) until prosciutto is crispy; the meat will then be cooked to medium. Grill mushrooms over direct heat for 4–5 minutes per side and serve with meat.

A country-style, upscale version of a barbecue classic: a meatball wrapped in bacon. Your guests will be amazed.

INGREDIENTS:

2 Tbsp (30 mL) dried apple slices, finely diced

2–4 Tbsp (30–60 mL) gin

1 lb (500 g) very fresh ground venison

2 tsp (10 mL) salt

1 tsp (5 mL) pepper

1 tsp (5 mL) ground dried oregano

4 slices wild boar bacon, smoked (or more, depending on the number of meatballs you wish to wrap)

YOU'LL ALSO NEED:

2 planks, pre-soaked in water for at least 5 hours

wild moinks

Soak apple pieces in gin for 1 hour. Blend meat, salt and spices well, mix in apple, and form mixture into 12 equally sized balls. Wrap 4 of them with the bacon strips, or more if desired. Place balls on planks and, using indirect heat, grill at 400°F (200°C) for about 30 minutes.

TIP: Serve with a dip of wild cranberry jam seasoned with long pepper and chili.

grilled radicchio

INGREDIENTS:

6 Tbsp (90 mL) pumpkin seed oil
2 Tbsp (30 mL) balsamic vinegar
1 Tbsp (15 mL) apple cider vinegar
3 Tbsp (45 mL) honey
2 cloves garlic, crushed
1 tsp (5 mL) salt
1 tsp (5 mL) pepper
4 small heads Treviso radicchio

Make a marinade from oil, vinegars, honey, garlic, salt and pepper. Cut radicchio in half, brush cut side with marinade, and let sit briefly for flavours to be absorbed. Grill cut-side down over direct heat at about 400°F (200°C), until the radicchios begin to collapse. Remove from grill and brush cut sides with marinade again—done.

wild boar filet

INGREDIENTS:

1 tsp (5 mL) paprika

1 tsp (5 mL) Ras el Hanout

1/2 tsp (2 mL) ground
caraway seed

1/2 tsp (2 mL) ground cloves

1 tsp (5 mL) salt

2 wild boar filets

2 Tbsp (30 mL) walnut oil

Thoroughly combine spices and salt. Rub filets with oil, then season with spice blend. Let sit 1–2 hours for seasonings to be absorbed. Using indirect heat in a charcoal or gas grill, slow roast with lid closed at about 250–275°F (120–140°C) for about 1 1/2 hours to an internal temperature of 135–140°F (58–60°C). If desired, also use smoke.

chili pears

INGREDIENTS:

1 Tbsp (15 mL) butter

4 pears, quartered and cored

2 medium chili peppers, finely chopped

salt, to taste

Melt butter in wok. Add pears and fry over high heat for about 5 minutes. Season to taste with chili peppers and salt.

Place Dutch oven on 20 glowing briquettes and heat olive oil in it. Sauté onion with tomato paste. Add meat, vegetables, herbs, wine, broth and puréed tomatoes. Cover, place 12 further briquettes on lid, and simmer for about 2 hours until meat is tender.

Remove meat, bay leaves and rosemary. Purée sauce and, if desired, season to taste with truffle salt and pepper. Serve meat in sauce.

hunter's wife roe deer
in a dutch oven

INGREDIENTS:

6 Tbsp (90 mL) olive oil

1 onion, finely chopped

3 Tbsp (45 mL) tomato paste

1 lb (500 g) roe deer shoulder, cut into cubes

1 carrot, washed and cut into pieces

1 stalk celery, washed and coarsely chopped

2 garlic cloves, halved

1 sprig fresh rosemary

2 bay leaves

3 cups (750 mL) red wine

2 cups (500 mL) meat broth (any kind from red meat will do)

1 can puréed tomatoes

truffle salt or salt, to taste (optional)

freshly ground pepper, to taste

YOU WILL ALSO NEED:

32 briquettes

Served in a cup, this also works as an appetizer.

venison with root vegetables

Lay meat out flat. Distribute parsnip, beet and oregano on it. Roll together and tie with kitchen string. Combine salt and spices. Rub meat with gin, then season with spice blend. Using indirect heat, grill at 250–275°F (120–140°C) for about 1 hour to an internal temperature of 155°F (68°C).

INGREDIENTS:

one 1 lb (500 g) boneless venison shoulder
1 parsnip, julienned
1 yellow carrot, julienned
1 sprig oregano
1 tsp (5 mL) salt
1 tsp (5 mL) black pepper
1 tsp (5 mL) smoked paprika
1 tsp (5 mL) ground caraway seed
1 tsp (5 mL) ground dried oregano
2 Tbsp (30 mL) gin

YOU'LL ALSO NEED:

kitchen string

venison steak

Pat entrecôte dry and grill at a high temperature over direct heat until meat releases juices. Turn meat and repeat. Wrap meat in aluminum foil and let rest in a warm place for 3–5 minutes. Season with salt and Indonesian long pepper.

INGREDIENTS:

1 venison entrecôte, at least
1 1/4 inches (3 cm) thick, per person
salt, to taste
Indonesian long pepper, crushed with mortar and pestle

YOU'LL ALSO NEED:

aluminum foil

133

grillwerkstattbohnen
in a dutch oven

INGREDIENTS:

7 oz (200 g) speck, finely diced

1 onion, chopped

3 cloves garlic, finely chopped

3 cups (750 mL) vegetable or
beef broth

4 lb 6 oz (2 kg) white kidney beans,
soaked for 24 hours

6 Tbsp (90 mL) brown sugar

2 cups (500 mL) ketchup

3/4 cup (185 mL) barbecue sauce

1 tsp (5 mL) salt

1 tsp (5 mL) pepper

1 tsp (5 mL) chili powder

YOU WILL ALSO NEED:

25 charcoal briquettes

Place 10 glowing briquettes under Dutch oven. Render speck in Dutch oven, add onion and garlic, and deglaze with broth. Drain beans and add to speck mixture along with sugar, ketchup and barbecue sauce. Cover, place 15 further briquettes on lid, and simmer for about 2 hours. Before serving, season to taste with salt, pepper and chili powder.

chili red cabbage

INGREDIENTS:

3 Tbsp (45 mL) olive oil

1 onion, finely chopped

1 red cabbage

2 cups (500 mL) red wine

1 fresh chili pepper, finely chopped

1/4 cup (60 mL) balsamic vinegar

salt, to taste

pepper, to taste

Heat oil in wok and fry onion until transparent. Thinly slice red cabbage and add to onions. Fry briefly, then deglaze with wine. Cook until al dente, stirring constantly. Season to taste with chili pepper, vinegar, salt and pepper.

a sweet ending

Cut off top third of each apple. Using a melon baller, scoop out middle and drizzle with Alpenbitter. Stuff each apple with a chocolate truffle, top with grated lebkuchen and walnuts, and sprinkle with lebkuchen spice. Using indirect heat, grill at 350–400°F (180–200°C) for about 30 minutes. Serve with whipped cream and vanilla ice cream.

tom's winter apples

INGREDIENTS:

4 small apples

2 Tbsp + 2 tsp (40 mL) Appenzeller Alpenbitter

4 chocolate nougat truffles, a denser kind is best

2 Tbsp (30 mL) lebkuchen or gingerbread, finely grated

2 Tbsp (30 mL) grated walnuts

1 tsp (5 mL) lebkuchen or gingerbread spice

INGREDIENTS:

3 Tbsp (45 mL) butter

1 cup (250 mL) sugar

pith of 1 vanilla bean

2 Tbsp (30 mL) cocoa powder

5 eggs, separated

3–4 slices pumpernickel, crusts removed, soaked in milk

3/4 cup (185 mL) walnuts, crushed

3/4 cup (185 mL) bread crumbs

4 apples, peeled and sliced

5 Tbsp + 1 tsp (80 mL) Appenzeller Alpenbitter

chocolate nut cupcakes with appenzell apples

Cream butter with sugar, vanilla, cocoa and egg yolks until fluffy. Squeeze liquid out of pumpernickel and stir bread into mixture along with walnuts and bread crumbs. Beat egg whites until they form stiff peaks, then fold into mixture. Spoon into muffin cups and, using indirect heat, grill at about 400°F (200°C) for 30 minutes. Toss apple slices in Appenzeller Alpenbitter and serve with cupcakes.

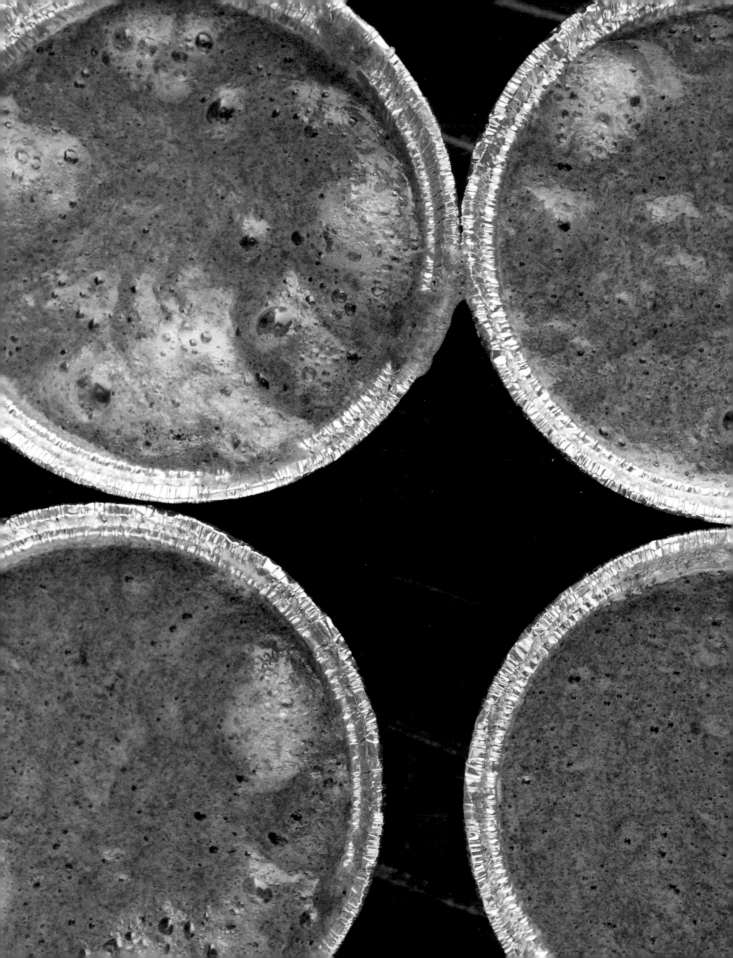

For this recipe, I like to use the black nuts that a friend of mine makes according to an age-old recipe: unripe green nuts are marinated for weeks in a special liquid, resulting in black, uniquely paltable nuts that can be used as an accompaniment for desserts and game dishes, and also in making ice cream.

INGREDIENTS PER PERSON:

2 fresh figs

6 Tbsp (90 mL) warm honey

1/4 cup (60 mL) syrup from 4 black nuts
(save the sliced nuts for serving)

1 tsp (5 mL) cinnamon

2 Tbsp (30 mL) brown sugar

grilled figs

Cut figs in half and brush cut surfaces with a mixture of warm honey, nut syrup and cinnamon. Briefly grill figs, cut-side down, over direct heat at 400°F (200°C). Serve with whipped cream, walnut ice cream and black nuts.

Dried fruits are very popular, especially in wintertime. I like to make a grilled version, with Irish whiskey lending the finishing touch.

dried fruit skewers with a shot

Thread dates and apricots onto skewers, alternating fruits, and marinate for about 2 hours in whiskey. Grill 3 minutes on each side over high heat.

INGREDIENTS:
40 dried dates
40 dried apricots
2/3 cup (160 mL) Irish whiskey

YOU'LL ALSO NEED:
8 wooden skewers, pre-soaked in water

Buchteln, sweet yeast dumplings, are one of my favourite desserts. I always fill them with jam made out of apricots from my own apricot trees (of the "Hungary's Best" variety), which thrive wonderfully in sheltered sunny spots in Vorarlberg, where I live.

buchteln
in a dutch oven

INGREDIENTS:

7 cups (1.75 L) cake flour
1 Tbsp (15 mL) dry yeast
1 1/4 cups (310 mL) warm milk
6 Tbsp (90 mL) granulated sugar
7 Tbsp (105 mL) butter
2 eggs
1 pinch salt
pith of 1 vanilla bean
10 oz (300 g) apricot jam
2 Tbsp (30 mL) confectioners' sugar

YOU WILL NEED:

20 charcoal briquettes

Combine flour, yeast, milk, sugar, butter, eggs, salt and vanilla, and knead into a soft dough. On a floured work surface, roll dough out to a thickness of about 1 cm. Using a glass, cut into circles just under 3 inches (7–8 cm) in diameter. Place 1 tsp (5 mL) jam on each circle, and close them up. Arrange close together in a Dutch oven and cover. Place 10 glowing briquets on top of and 10 underneath Dutch oven and bake dumplings 30–40 minutes. Sprinkle with confectioners' sugar before serving.

Kaiserschmarrn is a classic of Austrian cuisine. My version in a cast-iron pan uses prunes and is an especially palatable interpretation of this dish.

kaiserchmarrn

Combine prunes, cinnamon and jam with brandy and allow to infuse for about 1 hour. Mix together egg yolks, flour, sugar and milk into a thick, smooth batter. Beat egg whites with a pinch of salt until they form stiff peaks, then fold into batter. On the grill, in a cast-iron pan over direct heat, melt butter until frothy. Pour in batter and, using indirect heat, bake at 325°F (160°C) for about 30 minutes. Pull apart into irregular pieces and brown lightly over direct heat. Sprinkle with sugar and serve with plum sauce.

INGREDIENTS:

3 1/2 oz (100 g) prunes
1/2 tsp (2 mL) ground cinnamon
1/4 cup (60 mL) plum jam
4 tsp (20 mL) plum brandy
5 eggs, separated
2 3/4 cups (685 mL) all-purpose flour
1/4 cup (60 mL) sugar, divided
2 3/4 cups (685 mL) milk
1 pinch of salt
3 Tbsp (45 mL) butter

glossary

APPENZELLER ALPENBITTER
This is a bitter alcoholic liqueur originating in Switzerland. The Appenzeller brand is made from a secret blend of 42 different herbs and spices. It can be used in cooking or served as a digestif after you have eaten. Check at local specialty liquor stores for this drink. There are other alpenbitters available commercially made in a similar style to this one if you cannot find Appenzeller, such as Alpenbitter No. 7.

ALPINE HERB HAY
In Austria, herbs are harvested from alpine meadows and dried for culinary purposes. This is not the same type of hay used in North American agriculture. You can order it from Austrian retailers online such as Heu-Henrich or try foraging for your own edible wild herbs and make your own variant of it. A mixture of summer savory, rosemary, thyme and basil is a suitable substitution.

ANGELICA ROOT
Angelica is a member of the parsley family grown for its roots and stalks. The use of angelica as a flavouring is relatively common in Europe, but you may need to visit European specialty grocers to find it in North America.

BLACK NUTS
Black nuts are a specific kind of sweet walnut made from green walnuts, similar to *marrons glacés.* They are soft and sweet, and prepared by soaking in water for several days and then cooking in syrup. They are preserved in the syrup for long periods of time.

BLOOD SAUSAGE
The Austrian version of blood sausage is typically made from pig's blood usually mixed with a grain, like barley. It is usually bought precooked.

EISBOCK
Eisbock is a strong ice beer, which is often as high as 10% in alcohol content by volume. If you cannot find a true eisbock, look for a high alcohol bock beer (a malty and dark beer of German origin that is lightly hopped).

GARAM MASALA
Garam masala is an Indian blend of spices which usually contains a combination of cumin, coriander, pepper, cinnamon, cloves, nutmeg, fennel, chilies and cardamom. You should be able to find it at most major grocery stores.

HARISSA
Harissa is a Tunisian hot spice paste made from hot chiles, oil, garlic, coriander and caraway. It can be used in Middle Eastern dishes or as a hot sauce to give a dish some spice. It is usually found at Middle Eastern or North African grocers.

INDONESIAN LONG PEPPER
Sometimes just called "long peppers" or "Javanese peppers," Indonesian long peppers look like long skinny pine cones and are used as a spice. They are most commonly used in Asian and African cuisine. They have a flavour similar to black pepper, but with an earthiness and a numbing aftertaste. They can be found at South Asian grocers or reputable spice merchants.

JUNIPER BERRY
These dark blue berries are very bitter and are not usually eaten fresh. They can be bought dried from most spice merchants and used in meats and sauces. If they are native to where you live you can harvest and dry them yourself.

KNODELBROT

These dried bread cubes are a German variation on croutons. You can find them at German specialty stores, or use small croutons in their place.

LAMB'S LETTUCE

Lamb's lettuce, sometimes referred to as corn salad, is a tender green that can be harvested wild in Europe and North America. It has dark narrow leaves and a unique tangy flavour. When in season it can be found in some farmers' markets and gourmet produce stores. When stored it should be used within a day or two of acquiring, as it does not keep well.

LEBKUCHEN

This is a German Christmas treat similar to gingerbread. It can be found at German bakeries or grocers. If you are unable to find this you can substitute gingerbread for it, and gingerbread spice for lebkuchen spice.

MONTAFON SURA KEES

This cheese is a regional specialty of the Austrian valley of Montafon. It's a curdled milk cheese that is low in fat and slightly sour with a firm consistency. You may be able to find it at German or Austrian grocers or in specialty cheese stores. If you are unable to find it you can use a good quality feta cheese instead.

MUGWORT

Mugwort is a bitter flavouring agent that can be used to season many dishes. Before the use of hops it was sometimes used as a bittering agent in beers. It is particularly well suited to seasoning fatty meats.

MUSHROOMS

Many types of wild mushrooms are well suited to the recipes in this book. Just be sure to learn how to recognize edible wild mushrooms from an expert. Some of the recipes in this book call for king oyster mushrooms, also known as French horn mushrooms. This kind of mushroom may be difficult to find fresh in North America. If you are unable to find it, use whatever mushroom you like best. Porcini mushrooms are also used in this book and can be found at most gourmet produce or grocery stores.

PAPRIKA

This spice is made from grinding a variety of kinds of red peppers. European cooks have access to many different types of paprika spice not found in North American grocery stores. If attempting to find sweet paprika or hot paprika your best bet is an Eastern European grocer or a spice merchant.

RAS EL HANOUT

This is a complex Moroccan spice blend that has many varieties, some containing over 50 ingredients. This spice blend can be found at most spice merchants or North African specialty stores.

ROE DEER

Roe deer produces a meat less gamey than traditional venison. Native to much of Europe and Asia, it is prized for its delicate flavour. Roe deer may be difficult to find in North America, but it can be ordered through some specialty butchers. Venison can be used in place of roe deer in the recipes provided in this book, though the flavour will be slightly stronger and more gamey.

SPECK

Speck is a style of bacon common to many Germanic countries. It is closer in nature to a cold-smoked ham or a prosciutto than what is typically called bacon in North American grocery stores. To find speck, try looking in a German, Dutch or Austrian grocer or a gourmet deli.

tom heinzle
the grill master

Thomas "Tom" Heinzle is married and the father of two wonderful sons. He lives in Vorarlberg, Austria's westernmost state, which borders both Switzerland and Germany.

He was infected with the grill virus many years ago and is, like so many of his colleagues in the grill circus, a career changer. He started out as a mechanical engineer, but it was as an ambitious amateur cook with an addiction to perfection that he found his way to the embers.

He came into this world with an innately good sense of taste and smell; as an unconventional thinker, he brings both traditional and innovative cuisine to the grill.

So it's no wonder that, time and time again, his fascination with outstanding quality and his great respect for food results in unique recipes. Together with the team at his grill workshop (Tom's Grillwerkstatt, www.grillwerkstatt.at), Tom Heinzle regularly takes part in barbecue championships, where he's been named runner-up world champion more than once as well as Austrian national champion.

michael gunz
the photographer

Michael Gunz lives in beautiful Emsreute in the Vorarlberg part of Austria. Together with his wife and two sons, he enjoys a unique view of the Rhine valley from which he constantly derives the inspiration and vision that are so important in his profession.

His almost unbelievable energy and unconditional insistence on the very best are no accident: Michael Gunz was a competitive athlete, and this has left its stamp on the likeable man from Vorarlberg. In his quest for the perfect photo, his team spirit and focus on the essential stand him in good stead. He says of himself that he wants to bring out the distinctiveness of every product. The perfect photo begins with the craft of lighting—of which, as this book proves, he is a master—and doesn't end until the professional digital image processing has been completed.

But watch out: Michael can work to perfection faster than almost anyone on a grill . . . except for Tom.

I recommend the following companies and thank them for their support:

Appenzeller Alpenbitter
www.appenzeller.com

Mohrenbräu Dornbirn
www.mohrenbrauerei.at

Napoleon Gourmetgrills
www.napoleongrills.eu

Smoky Fun
www.smokyfun.eu

Schobel Höchstgenuss Trockenfrüchte
www.hoechstgenuss.at